# this is my faith

# Hinduism

by Holly Wallace

## BARRON'S

First edition for the United States, its territories and dependencies, Canada,
and the Philippine Republic published in 2006 by Barron's Educational Series, Inc.

First published in Great Britain in 2006 by ticktock Media Ltd.,
Unit 2, Orchard Business Centre, North Farm Road, Tunbridge Wells, Kent, TN2 3XF

All inquiries should be addressed to:
Barron's Educational Series, Inc.
250 Wireless Boulevard
Hauppauge, NY 11788
**www.barronseduc.com**

ISBN-13: 978-0-7641-5965-7 (Hardcover)
ISBN-10: 0-7641-5965-8 (Hardcover)

ISBN-13: 978-0-7641-3474-6 (Paperback)
ISBN-10: 0-7641-3474-4 (Paperback)

Library of Congress Control Number: 2005939034

Picture credits
t = top, b = bottom, c = center, l = left, r = right,
OFC = outside front cover, OBC = outside back cover

Alamy: 9t, 11c.  Corbis: 9c, 9b, 23b, 25b, 24main, 26main.  Getty: 27b.  Plan UK and Plan International: OFC,
1, 2, 4b, 5-7all, 10, 12b, 14-17all, 18t, 20all, 22all, 24t, 27c, 31tr, OBC. Shutterstock: 18b, 30t, 31tl.
Superstock: 11b, 19t. World Religions PL/ Christine Osborne: (Nick Dawson: 11t, 19c) 13t, 13b, 19b, 21c,
(Prem Kapoor: 21t, 21b, 23t, 25c), (GB. Mukherji: 23c), 25t.

Every effort has been made to trace the copyright holders, and we apologize in advance for any unintentional omissions.
We would be pleased to insert the appropriate acknowledgments in any subsequent edition of this book.

Printed in China
9 8 7 6 5 4 3 2 1

# Contents

I am a Hindu . . . . . . . . . . . . . . . . . . 4-5

My family . . . . . . . . . . . . . . . . . . . 6-7

LEARN MORE: What is Hinduism? . . . . . . . . 8-9

What I believe . . . . . . . . . . . . . . . . .10-11

LEARN MORE: The holiest books . . . . . . . .12-13

Family Gods . . . . . . . . . . . . . . . . . .14-15

Where I worship . . . . . . . . . . . . . . . .16-17

Worshipping at home . . . . . . . . . . . . . .18-19

Diwali—festival of lights . . . . . . . . . . . .20-21

Holi—festival of colors . . . . . . . . . . . .22-23

Other festivals . . . . . . . . . . . . . . . . .24-25

Special occasions . . . . . . . . . . . . . . . .26-27

LEARN MORE: Holy places . . . . . . . . . . . .28-29

Glossary . . . . . . . . . . . . . . . . . . .30-31

Index . . . . . . . . . . . . . . . . . . . . .32

Words that appear in **bold** are explained in the glossary.

# I am a Hindu

"My name is Babu and I am 10 years old. I live in a village in Nepal. My family and I follow the religion of **Hinduism**. We are **Hindus**."

"Hinduism teaches me that my soul, the real me, is **eternal**. My soul is different from my body, which will die one day. The soul is there in all creatures so we must respect all people, and animals, too."

This is Babu. The red mark on her forehead is called a **tilak**. It is a sign of God's protection.

This is where Babu lives. Her house is in a quiet village near Kathmandu, in Nepal.

"This is my house. It is made from stone, brick, and wood and it has four bedrooms."

"When Hindus greet each other, we put the palms of our hands together and say 'Namaste.'"

"Namaste" comes from the ancient Indian language of **Sanskrit**. It means "My respects to you."

Om is believed to be the sign and sound of creation, and of the whole **Universe**.

"This is the Om **symbol**. It is often used as the sign of Hinduism. 'Om' is also a sacred sound that we say at the beginning and end of many prayers."

# My family

"I live with my family. I have a mother and father, and a younger brother and little sister."

"I live just like any other child but I try to be a good Hindu, too. That means living in the way that God wants me to. Every day, I try to spend time saying my prayers."

This is my grandfather, Arjun.

This is my grandmother, Riya.

This is me, Babu.

This is my brother, Anup.

This is my mother, Chandra.

This is my father, Hem.

This is my sister, Nnita.

Hindu children are taught to be polite to their parents and grandparents.

"We believe that it is important to love and obey our elders. When we meet, we often touch their feet to show respect."

"Before we eat our meal, we offer some of our food to God. Many Hindus are **vegetarians** so we don't eat meat."

Babu's family eat a meal of vegetables and rice. Hindus believe it is wrong to kill or harm living things.

Babu prepares to go to her local school. As a Hindu, she is brought up to work hard.

"It is important to work hard, whether this means in the fields, in a factory, or in an office-or at school!"

7

# LEARN MORE: What is Hinduism?

- Hinduism is one of the world's oldest religions. It is at least 5,000 years old. Most Hindus live in India and other Asian countries, like Nepal and Indonesia. But there are also a lot of Hindus in Europe, North America, and Africa.

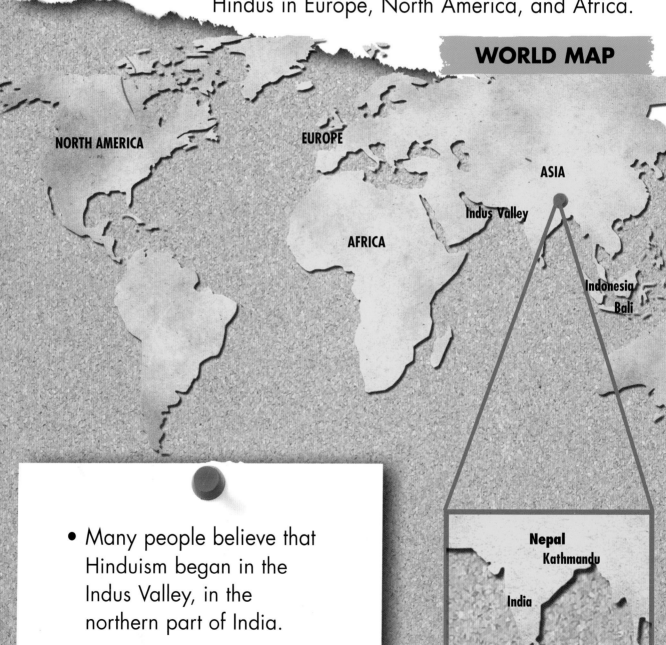

**WORLD MAP**

NORTH AMERICA

EUROPE

ASIA

Indus Valley

AFRICA

Indonesia
Bali

Nepal
Kathmandu

India

- Many people believe that Hinduism began in the Indus Valley, in the northern part of India.

Many Hindus worship in places called **mandirs**. The English word for mandir is "temple." There are thousands of mandirs all over India.

Part of the colorful Kapaleeshwara Temple in Madras, India.

• Hindus believe in four main **deities**: Brahma the creator; Vishnu the protector; Shiva the destroyer; and Shiva's wife, Shakti (also called Durga and Parvati).

In Bali, colorful dances and puppet shows are used to tell **sacred** stories.

• On the island of Bali, in Indonesia, most of the people are Hindus. Hinduism was brought to Bali from India, by traders about 1,800 years ago.

# What I believe

"Hindus believe in an invisible, eternal spirit called Brahman. Some Hindus call Brahman 'God.'"

"Hindus believe that the soul is a part of God and is also eternal. When we die, we enter another body, as a person, or as a plant or animal. What the new body is depends on how good we have been in this life. This is called **reincarnation**."

**Like other Hindus, Babu believes that if we are really good, we become united with God and escape the cycle of reincarnation. Hindus unite with God through worship and meditation.**

Young girls have the tilak put on their forehead at many special occasions.

"During the worship, the tilak is made on everyone's forehead. It is made from special red powder and is a sign of God's blessing."

"When we enter a mandir, we ring the temple bell loudly. The sound wakes up our senses so that we can worship God."

In Hindu temples there is usually a sacred statue of one of the Hindu deities. Ringing the bell lets the deity know you are there.

When Hindus get older and retire, many become sadhus. This sadhu is praying and **meditating** outside a temple.

"**Sadhus** are very **devout** Hindus. They give up their homes and everything they own to concentrate their minds on God."

# LEARN MORE:
## The holiest books

• Hindus have many holy books. Some of them tell stories about the deities and how to worship them. Others teach about right and wrong, and how to live as a good Hindu.

• Most Hindu holy books were written down in an ancient language called Sanskrit. This is a sacred language. The holy books are very difficult for most people to understand. Hindu priests study them and explain their meaning.

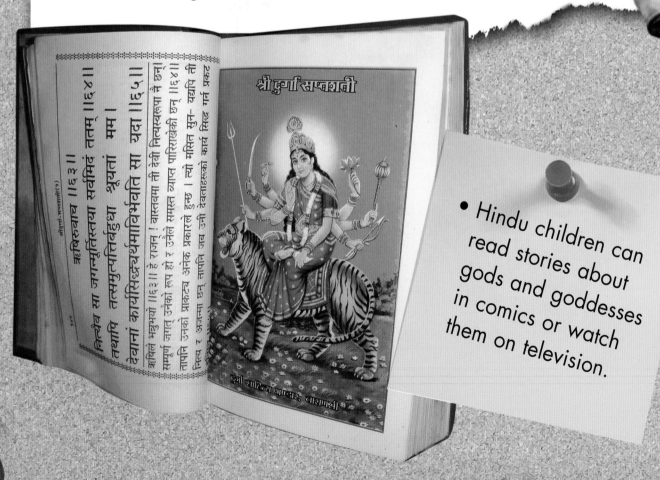

• Hindu children can read stories about gods and goddesses in comics or watch them on television.

The Ramayana is often acted on stage. This is a performance in Bali.

A Hindu reads from a prayer book in Varanasi, India.

The holy book called the Mahabharata tells the story of Lord Krishna. This picture shows part of the story when Krishna goes into battle, on his chariot pulled by white horses.

- The Ramayana is a holy book. It tells the story of Lord Rama and his wife Sita. Rama's stepmother sent them to live in the forest so that she could make her own son king. In the forest, Sita was kidnapped by a **demon** called Ravana, but she was rescued by Rama and Hanuman, the monkey warrior. Sita and Rama returned home and were crowned king and queen.

# Family Gods

"Most Hindu families choose certain deities that they worship. They have pictures or holy statues of these deities in their **shrine** at home."

"My family worships Lord Shiva, who destroys evil and protects us from pain and suffering."

**Lord Shiva is often shown dancing, or sitting in meditation.**

In holy statues and paintings Krishna is often shown with a cow and playing the flute.

"One of the most popular deities is Krishna. He is worshipped all over India. He is a warrior and a teacher."

"Shakti is usually gentle and kind, but sometimes she is fierce. In her fierce form, she is called Durga. She is armed with weapons and rides a lion or a tiger."

The main Hindu goddess is called Shakti. Here she is shown as Durga.

Pictures and statues of Lakshmi are often seen in shops and businesses, to help them be successful.

"My favorite deity is Lakshmi. This is because she is the goddess of good luck and wealth."

# Where I worship

"Every week, I go to a mandir near my home dedicated to Lord Shiva and his wife, Shakti, who is also called Parvati."

"When we go to the mandir, we do **puja**. This is the Hindu word for worship. We make offerings and in return we hope to receive the blessing of Lord Shiva."

**Babu and her younger brother enjoy doing puja at the temple.**

The sacred stone column represents Lord Shiva.

"My brother and I do puja to show our love and respect for God. We put our hands together as we say our prayers."

"I often offer a basket of red flowers to God. Sometimes we offer fruit, rice, **incense**, or gifts of money."

Hindus make offerings as a sign of love for God. Babu makes hers with great care.

This stone carving of Ganesh is inside Archana's local mandir. Ganesh is the god of beginnings.

"Ganesh is the elephant-headed god. He is the son of Shiva and Parvati. We worship him when we start anything new, like moving into a new house."

# Worshipping at home

"I worship every day with my family at home. We have a puja room in our house, with pictures of the deities we pray to."

"We do puja there early in the morning, usually at around 7 or 8 o'clock. Doing puja means I start each day with God's blessing."

**Early morning is a good time for puja, when the house is quiet.**

Puja uses the five senses. Looking at the sacred images uses sight, and singing songs to the gods uses sound.

"In our puja room, we have paintings of several different deities, including Shiva, Parvati, Ganesh, and Lakshmi."

"We give offerings to the deities on a plate. These include flowers, rice, red powder for tilak, and wicks to light the oil lamp."

Food is offered during puja and eaten later. This uses the senses of taste and touch.

When the incense sticks are lit, Babu is using her sense of smell.

"I light some sticks of **incense** to give a pleasant smell. It is also a way of welcoming God."

19

# Diwali—festival of lights

"Our most important festival is Diwali. In Nepal, we call the festival Tihar. This festival celebrates the homecoming of Rama and Sita from the forest. It also welcomes the goddess Lakshmi into our homes."

"We clean our houses and wear our best clothes. Sometimes we get new clothes."

During Tihar, children from Babu's village light little lamps and go from door to door, singing and dancing. People give money, fruit, and rice in return.

In some places Hindus float their candles on water. This little girl is setting her candle afloat on the River Ganges.

"Diwali marks the victory of light over darkness, and good over evil. We celebrate by lighting up our homes and mandirs with lots of candles."

"At Tihar, I also give my older brother garlands and sweets. In return, he gives me some money."

Diwali is celebrated in October or November. Some people send special Diwali cards to their friends and family.

Rangoli patterns are usually in the shapes of flowers and leaves. These patterns and lights are to welcome the goddess Lakshmi into the home.

"At the beginning of Tihar many Hindus make **rangoli** patterns on their doorstep, or in front of the house. These are made with rice powder, flour, and water."

# Holi—festival of colors

"Holi is a festival that marks the beginning of spring and remembers the story of the wicked Holika, who wanted to get rid of her nephew, Prince Prahlad."

"Holika had a special power and could not be harmed by fire. But when she tried to burn Prince Prahlad to death, he stepped from the fire unharmed and Holika's power was broken. She burned to death instead."

Babu enjoys hearing the story of Prince Prahlad and his wicked aunt, Holika. The story shows how Krishna protects good people and destroys evil.

Everyone helps to make a bonfire to begin the Holi celebrations.

"We build a bonfire on the first day of Holi to remember the end of Holika's powers and the victory of good over evil."

"As part of the fun, we throw colored powder over each other. We use bright colors like orange, red, and blue."

A Hindu priest joins in the Holi fun. It is a festival for everyone to enjoy.

Children buy water guns to play with during Holi. Nobody minds getting wet as it is so hot.

"We also throw water over each other. This is to remind us of stories about Krishna splashing in the river during springtime."

# Other festivals

"There are many other Hindu festivals. Most celebrate important events in the lives of deities. These times are always fun and I enjoy them with my family."

"Durga Puja is a festival which lasts for nine days. At this this time we remember how Durga killed a demon, who took the form of a giant buffalo. It shows that good will win over evil."

During the festival of Durga Puja the story of Durga is often performed. Durga is shown with ten arms and riding a lion. She is like a mother who becomes angry to protect her children.

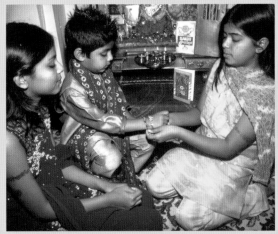

The festival of Raksha Bandhan is for brothers and sisters. Brothers promise to love and care for their sisters.

"In August, we celebrate the festival of Raksha Bandhan. I tie a brightly colored bracelet around my brother's wrist."

"We celebrate Lord Krishna's birthday in August or September at the festival of Janmashtami. Stories from Krishna's life are acted out in the mandir."

As part of the festival, an image of baby Krishna is put in a cradle or swing and decorated with flowers and garlands.

The festival of Ganesh's birthday is very popular with Hindus in Mumbai, in India.

"The festival marking the god Ganesh's birthday lasts for eleven days. Crowds of Hindus carry very big holy statues of Ganesh to the sea."

25

# Special occasions

"There are many special times when my family gets together to celebrate at home or in the mandir."

"When my brother was born, he was washed and then my father put a few drops of **ghee** and honey in his mouth. We all said prayers. When he was 11 days old, he was named and more prayers were said."

At the age of one, a baby has its first haircut. A Hindu priest rings a temple bell during the ceremony.

Hindus wear the sacred thread over the left shoulder, and wrapped around the right thumb, when they say their prayers.

"When my brothers are ten years old they will be given a **sacred thread** to wear which marks the start of their adult life."

"A Hindu wedding ceremony takes place around a sacred fire. The couple takes seven steps together and make a promise at each step."

The bride usually wears a beautiful red sari, and lots of makeup and jewelry.

In India, many bodies are cremated along the River Ganges, the most holy river for Hindus.

"When a Hindu dies, his or her body is washed and dressed in fresh clothes. In India, relatives carry the body to the river where it is **cremated**."

# LEARN MORE: *Holy places*

- The holiest place for many Hindus is the city of Varanasi in northern India. Millions of pilgrims visit this city to bathe in the sacred River Ganges.

- Some Hindu holy sites are places once visited by one of the deities. Today, there are often temples there to mark the spot.

- Pashupathinath is a place in Kathmandu, in Nepal, which was visited by Lord Shiva as a place to rest. It is visited by many Hindus.

- Those who make the journey to Pashupathinath often pray for something special, such as good health or good luck on a long journey.

People have been worshipping at the mandir at Pashupathinath for nearly 1,500 years.

Hindus believe the River Ganges started life as the goddess Ganga, before being brought to Earth by King Bhagiratha. Every day Hindus can be seen bathing in the sacred waters.

• Mount Kailash in the Himalayan mountains is believed to be Lord Shiva's home on Earth. The Himalayas stretch across the north of India and through Nepal.

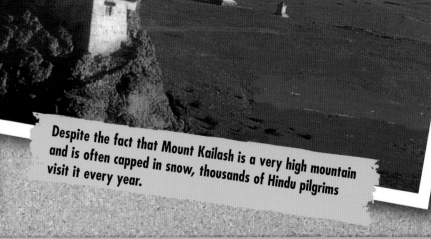

Despite the fact that Mount Kailash is a very high mountain and is often capped in snow, thousands of Hindu pilgrims visit it every year.

# Glossary

**Incense**

**Brahman** The great power or spirit that is everywhere.

**Ceremony** An act or set of religious acts.

**Cremated** When a dead person's body is burned.

**Dedicated** "Dedicated to" means "special to."

**Deities** Forms of God, or of a particular god or goddess.

**Demon** An evil spirit.

**Devout** Very religious.

**Eternal** Lasting forever. Without a beginning or an end.

**Ghee** A type of oil made from butter used in Indian cooking.

**Hinduism** The religion of people called Hindus.

**Hindus** People who follow the religion of Hinduism.

**Incense** Sticks of sweet-smelling spices and perfume burned in temples and shrines.

**Mandir** An Indian word for temple, where many Hindus worship.

**Meditation** To sit quietly to clear and concentrate your mind so that you feel calm and relaxed.

**Namaste** An Indian greeting. Namaste means "my respects to you." Hindus put the palms of their hands together when they say "Namaste."

**Om** A sacred symbol used in many prayers. The symbol is used to represent Hinduism.

**Pilgrimages** Journeys to holy places such as mandirs or sacred rivers. Hindus make these journeys to become closer to God.

**Puja** The main Hindu form of worship. It means "giving respect."

**Ghee**

**Om**

**Rangoli** A type of art that is very popular in India. It is made up of brightly colored patterns. It is usually used to decorate the outside of the home at Diwali.

**Reincarnation** The belief that when we die, we leave this body and enter another one. We pass through many lives as a human, animal, or plant. This goes on until we are united with God.

**Sacred** Another word for holy.

**Sacred thread** A cotton thread that is worn over the left shoulder and that is used during prayer.

**Sadhu** A Hindu holy man.

**Sanskrit** An ancient Indian language. Many holy books were first written in Sanskrit. For Hindus, it is still the most important language for prayer and worship.

**Shrine** A place that has a holy statue or image of a Hindu god or goddess and that is used for prayer.

**Symbol** An object or sign that has a special meaning and that stands for something else.

**Tilak** A mark made of paste, ash, or red powder, put on the forehead.

**Universe** Everything on Earth and in space.

**Vegetarians** People who do not eat meat or fish.

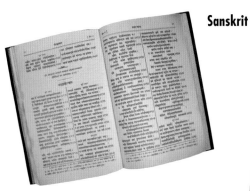

**Sanskrit**

**Namaste**

# Index

**B**

beliefs 10–11
blessings 16, 18
bonfire 23
Brahma 9
Brahman 10, 30

**C**

ceremonies 30
colored powder 23
cremated bodies 27, 30

**D**

dedicated 30
deities 9, 24–25, 30
demons 13, 30
devout 11, 30
Diwali 20–21
Durga 9, 15, 24
Durga Puja 24

**E**

elephant-headed god 17
eternal 4, 10, 30

**F**

family gods 14–15
festival of colors 22–23
festival of lights 20–21
festivals 20–21, 22–23, 24–25

**G**

Ganesh 17, 19, 25
garlands 21
ghee 26, 30
God 6–7, 10

**H**

Hinduism 4, 8–9, 30
Hindus 4, 30
Holi 22–23
Holika 22
holy books 12–13
holy places 28–29

**I**

incense 17, 19, 30

**J**

Janmashtami 25

**K**

Krishna 13, 15, 23, 25

**L**

Lakshmi 15, 19, 20

**M**

Mahabharata 13
mandirs 9, 11, 16, 25, 30
meditation 10, 11, 30

**N**

Namaste 5, 30

**O**

offerings 19
Om symbol 5, 30

**P**

Parvati 9, 16–17, 19
Pashupathinath 28–29
pilgrimage 29, 30
prayers 5, 6, 17
Prince Prahlad 22
puja 16–17, 18–19, 31

**R**

Raksha Bandhan 25
Rama 13, 20
Ramayana 13

rangoli 31
rangoli patterns 21
reincarnation 10, 31
respect 4, 7, 17
River Ganges 21, 27, 28–29

**S**

sacred 31
sacred fire 27
sacred thread 27, 31
sadhu 31
sadhus 11
Sanskrit language 5, 12, 31
senses 19
Shakti 9, 15, 16–17
Shiva 9, 14, 16–17, 19
shrine 14, 31
Sita 13, 20
soul 4, 10
special occasions 26–27
symbols 5, 31

**T**

temples 9, 11
Tihar 20–21
tilak 4, 11, 19, 31

**U**

universe 5, 31

**V**

Varanasi 28
vegetarians 6, 31
Vishnu 9

**W**

weddings 27
worship 16–19